Easy Keto Desserts Cookbook:

Delicious Ketogenic Dessert Recipes For Weight Loss

circumstances will any legal obligation or blame be held against the publisher for any reparation, damages, or monetary loss due to the information herein, either directly or indirectly.

Respective authors own all copyrights not held by the publisher.

The information herein is offered for informational purposes solely and is universal as so. The presentation of the information is without a contract or any guarantee assurance.

The trademarks that are used are without any consent, and the publication of the trademark is without permission or backing by the trademark owner. All trademarks and brands within this book are for clarifying purposes only and are owned by the owners themselves, not affiliated with this document.

Table of Contents

Ketogenic Desserts 10

   Why Keto Desserts? 10

Ketogenic Dessert Recipes 14

Cake Recipes 14

   Buttery Chocolate Cake..14

   Zesty Lemon Cake 17

   Citrus Cream Cake...20

   Chunky Carrot Cake 23

   Layered Cream Cake..26

   Double layer Cream Cake 29

   Italian Pecan Cake 32

   Allspice Almond Cake...36

Keto bar Recipes...39

   Crunchy Chocolate Bars 39

   Lemon Egg Bars 41

   Caramel Bars 43

   Peanut Butter Bars 46

   Chocolate Dipped Granola Bars................................48

   Lime Mixed Shortbread Bars......................................51

   Chocolate Protein Bar...54

   Sukrin Protein Bars 56

Pie and Tart Recipes...59

   Mixed Berries Tart...59

   Creamy Chocolate Tart..62

   Blackberry Lemon Tart..65

   Strawberry Vanilla Tart 67

Blueberry Lemon Filling Tart...70

Cheesecake Jam Tarts 73

Pumpkin Almond Pie 76

Almond Meal Vanilla Tart 79

Cookie Recipes 82

Chocolate Chip Butter Cookies 82

Vanilla Shortbread Cookies..84

Cream Dipped Cookies..86

Nutmeg Gingersnap Cookies 89

Buttery Energy Bites 91

Cinnamon Snickerdoodle Balls.....................................93

Vanilla Cream Cheese Cookies......................................96

Coconut Vanilla Cookies 98

Candy and Confections 100

Raspberry Fat Bombs 100

Peppermint Candies 102

Cocoa Peppermint Fat Bombs 104

Coconut Tea Candy..106

Cucumber and Lime Sweets 108

Hibiscus Gelatin Gummies 110

Turmeric Milk Gummies...112

Cinnamon Pecans Candies 114

Frozen Desserts..116

Vanilla Yogurt..116

Mango yogurt popsicles 118

Protein yogurt 120

Cocoa Yogurt Ice Cream 122

Frozen yogurt with Berries 124

Raspberry Ice cream 126

Creamy Avocado Dessert 128

Cheesecake Vanilla Bites 130

Custard or Mousse Recipes 132

Vanilla custard with Pecan 132

Lemon Cream Custard 134

Vanilla Bean Custard 136

Vanilla Crème Brûlée 138

Coconut Chocolate Mousse 140

Raspberry Pecan Mousse..142

Cocoa Mocha Mousse 144

Conclusion 146

Ketogenic Desserts

The world has shifted to keto-trend. This is planning. It's all about your food routine and gives you a noticeable output. The question arises; what is that output?

Answer to the question that this diet called keto diet helps you to get rid of extra body fats and helps you to look smarter. The basic idea of bringing the body into ketosis is providing it with excessive fats and keeping carbohydrates low. Then the human body burns those fats to gain energy and makes fuel that was previously being made by carbohydrates. Fats burnt, target achieved!

Sweets are liked by almost everyone regardless of their age. Whether they are infants, youngsters or older people, all of them love to eat sweets and can't give up sweets. It can be said that our meals are incomplete unless we add desserts to them. But for those people who are in a keto-diet plan must need to stay away from sweets as they contain many carbs. There is no need to be sad keto eaters because keto desserts are available for you!

Why Keto Desserts?

They contain a lot of fats in the creamy ingredients we always wish to eat. They are particularly prepared for those people who are following a keto-diet plan. Normally, sugar is the main ingredient responsible for making foods sweet, but it can't be added to keto desserts. The problem is resolved by adding other sweeteners that replace sugar. Keto desserts are a treat for you guys. The dessert recipes are delicious and at the same time suitable for a ketogenic diet. What else would you demand then!

Keto desserts are those yummy sweet dishes that you are compelled to eat. These are a true gift for keto beginners because it is most difficult for them to give up sweets all of a sudden. The important thing to be noticed is the difference these desserts have from other sweet dishes. We use different sweeteners, flour substitutes, and specific fruits and dairy products avoiding all those items that are prohibited in a ketogenic diet plan.

What is the plan for milk and other dairy products while preparing keto desserts?

Keto eaters should not add dairy products to every meal they eat. However, dairy products can be taken on a regular basis. Milk is among the food ingredients of your keto desserts. Dieticians do not say to avoid milk in your keto diet plan which means that you can add milk to keto desserts. This addition must not be so lavish and do check your carb intake.

Milk may be added keeping in view your carb content and do not exceed the defined value. Milk you are taking must contain fats. It is not allowed to drink milk or eat ice-creams that do not contain fats. There are some dairy products which are completely fatty and are great for your keto diet plan. Other dairy products are those who give you lowest carbs. They include different types of cheeses, Greek yogurt, cream, and butter.

Replacements for keto-flours

Flours are always needed while baking something. Many dessert recipes need baking so it's complicated to decide what you would do to decrease your carb intake. Keto-flours provide you with fewest carbs and let you enjoy desserts at the same time. Let's have a look at keto-flours or flour replacements:

1. Ground Flax is used that can even replace eggs. Two tbsp of it will give you 1 gram net carbs.
2. Almond Flour is used that can be stored for a long time and quarter-filled cup of it gives you 3 grams net carbs.
3. Psyllium Husk gives you 1.5 grams net carb in each tablespoon.
4. Coconut Flour gives thickness to your dessert and provides few carbs only.

Some Sweeteners for keto desserts

Given below is the list of sweeteners that can be added to keto desserts. They can be added fearlessly to keto recipes because they do not contain a high content of carbohydrates. Let's name some commonly used replacements that are frequently added to keto desserts.

1. Stevia
2. Insulin-Based Sweeteners
3. Lucama Powder
4. Yacon Syrup
5. Monk Fruit Sweetener
6. Xylitol
7. Dark Chocolate
8. Erythritol
9. Tagatose

These sweeteners contain low carbohydrates or do not have carbs so are satisfactorily used in delicious keto sweet preparations.

Ketogenic Dessert Recipes

Cake Recipes

Buttery Chocolate Cake

Ingredients:

- 7 oz. sugar-free dark chocolate
- 3.5 oz. butter
- 3.4 oz. cream
- 4 egg whites
- 4 egg yolks
- erythritol to taste

Method:

1. Take an 8-inch baking pan and rub some butter in it to grease it.

2. Melt the remaining butter with chocolate in the microwave then mix well.

3. Once melted add cream and erythritol to the chocolate mixture.

4. Beat in egg yolks and beat until it is well incorporated.

5. Whisk egg white within another mixing bowl until it turns foamy.

6. Fold the egg white foam into the creamy butter mixture.

7. Use a spatula to transfer the batter to the prepared baking pan.

8. Bake it in the preheated oven for 45 minutes at 325 degrees F.

9. Remove the cake from the pan and place it over the wire rack.

10. Let it cool for 5 mins then refrigerate it for 4 hours packed in a plastic sheet.

11. Slice and serve the cake.

Prep Time: 15 minutes
Cooking Time: 46 minutes
Total Time: 61 minutes
Serving: 6

Nutritional Values:

- *Calories 173*
- *Total Fat 16.2 g*
- *Saturated Fat 9.8 g*
- *Cholesterol 100 mg*
- *Sodium 42 mg*
- *Total Carbs 9.4 g*
- *Sugar 0.2 g*
- *Fibre1 g*
- *Protein 3.3 g*

Zesty Lemon Cake

Ingredients:

Cake

- 1/2 cup coconut flour
- 5 eggs
- 1/4 cup Swerve
- 1/2 cup butter, melted
- Juice from 1/2 lemon
- 1/2 teaspoon lemon zest
- 1/2 teaspoon xanthan gum
- 1/2 teaspoon salt

Icing

- 1 cup cream cheese
- 3 tablespoons swerve
- 1 teaspoon vanilla essence
- ½ teaspoon lemon zest

Method:

1. Whisk egg whites using an electric mixer until it forms stiff peaks.
2. Put everything else in another bowl and mix them well.
3. Once well-combined fold in egg white foam and whisk it gently.
4. Use a spatula to transfer the batter to a 9x5 inch loaf pan, greased with oil.
5. Bake the foamy batter in a preheated oven for 45 minutes at 335 degrees F.
6. Meanwhile, prepare the topping by beating icing ingredients in the electric mixer.
7. Place the baked cake on the wire rack and let it cool for 10 minutes.
8. Spread the cream cheese icing over the cake and spread it evenly.
9. Refrigerate for 30 minutes or more.
10. Garnish as desired.
11. Slice and enjoy after a meal.

Prep Time: 15 minutes

Cooking Time: 45 minutes

Total Time: 60 minutes

Serving: 8

Nutritional Values:

- *Calories 251*
- *Total Fat 24.5 g*
- *Saturated Fat 14.7 g*
- *Cholesterol 165 mg*
- *Sodium 142 mg*
- *Total Carbs 4.3 g*
- *Sugar 0.5 g*
- *Fiber 1 g*
- *Protein 5.9 g*

Citrus Cream Cake

Ingredients:

Cake

- ¾ teaspoons vanilla essence
- 4 whole eggs
- ¼ cup butter, unsalted softened
- 1 ¼ cups almond flour
- 3/4 cup erythritol
- ¼ teaspoon lemon essence
- ¼ teaspoon salt
- 4 ounces cream cheese
- ¾ teaspoons baking powder

Cream Frosting

- 1/8 cup erythritol
- 1 ½ tablespoon heavy whipping cream
- ¼ teaspoon vanilla essence

Method:

1. Adjust the oven at 350 degrees F to preheat.
2. Meanwhile, beat butter with erythritol and cream cheese in a suitable bowl.
3. Stir in eggs, lemon essence and vanilla beat well.
4. Whisk in baking powder, salt, and almond flour.
5. Once the batter is combined well transfer it to a greased baking pan.
6. Bake the cake in preheated oven for 60 minutes at 350 degrees.
7. Beat all the ingredients for the frosting in a suitable bowl.
8. Once done, remove the cake from the pan and place it over the wire rack.
9. Let it cool for 10 mins then spread the cream frosting on its top.
10. Refrigerate the cake for 30 minutes or more.
11. Slice and serve to enjoy.

Prep Time: 15 minutes
Cooking Time: 60 minutes
Total Time: 75 minutes
Serving: 4

Nutritional Values:

- *Calories 255*
- *Total Fat 23.4 g*
- *Saturated Fat 11.7 g*
- *Cholesterol 135 mg*
- *Sodium 112 mg*
- *Total Carbs 2.5 g*
- *Sugar 12.5 g*
- *Fiber 1 g*
- *Protein 7.9 g*

Chunky Carrot Cake

Ingredients:

- 3/4 cup erythritol
- 3/4 cup butter
- 1 teaspoon vanilla essence
- 1/2 teaspoon pineapple extract
- 4 large egg
- 2 1/2 cup almond flour
- 2 teaspoons gluten-free baking powder
- 2 teaspoons cinnamon
- 1/2 teaspoon sea salt
- 2 1/2 cup carrots, grated

- 1 cup pecans, chopped
- Pecans, to garnish

Method:
1. Let your oven preheat at 350 degrees F.
2. Grease the base of two 9 inch baking dishes and layer it with parchment paper.
3. Beat erythritol in cream in a suitable bowl.
4. Stir in vanilla essence and pineapple extract.
5. While beating this mixture start adding eggs one by one.
6. Add cinnamon, salt, baking powder and flour in this mixture.
7. Whisk well to combine.
8. Fold in 1 cup chopped pecans and carrots.
9. Divide the entire batter in the two pans.
10. Bake them for 30 minutes in the preheated oven.
11. Remove both the cakes from the pans and let them cool for 10 minutes on wire racks.
12. Use the remaining pecans to garnish it.
13. Slice and serve.

Prep Time: 15 minutes
Cooking Time: 30 minutes
Total Time: 45 minutes
Serving: 8

Nutritional Values:

- *Calories 359*
- *Total Fat 34 g*
- *Saturated Fat 10.3 g*
- *Cholesterol 112 mg*
- *Sodium 92 mg*
- *Total Carbs 8.5 g*
- *Sugar 2 g*
- *Fiber 1.3 g*
- Protein 7.5 g

Layered Cream Cake

Ingredients:

Cream Cheese Icing:

- 8 oz. cream cheese softened
- 1/2 cup butter softened
- 1/2 cup powdered Swerve
- 1 teaspoon vanilla essence optional
- 2 tablespoons heavy cream

Carrot Cake Layers:

- 5 eggs large
- 3/4 cup erythritol
- 2 teaspoons vanilla essence
- 14 tablespoons butter melted
- 1/4 teaspoon unsweetened coconut, shredded

- 1/4 teaspoon salt
- 1/2 cup coconut flour
- 1 3/4 cup almond flour
- 2 teaspoons baking powder
- 1 1/2 teaspoon cinnamon, ground
- 1 1/4 cup shredded carrots

Method:

1. Beat all the ingredients for icing in an electric mixer until foamy. Set it aside.

For carrot cake layers:

2. Preheat your oven to 350 degrees F.
3. Lay the inside of two 8 inch baking pan with parchment paper.
4. Grease the baking pans and set them aside.
5. Beat eggs with erythritol in an electric mixer for 5 minutes until foamy.
6. Mix coconut flour, salt, almond flour, baking powder, and cinnamon.
7. Transfer this mixture to the egg batter and mix well until smooth.
8. Fold in coconut, butter, melted, and carrots. Stir well.
9. Divide the cake batter into two pans and bake for 30 minutes.
10. Allow them to cook for 10 to 15 minutes.

To Assemble:

11. Top 1 cake with half of the icing mixture.

12. Place another cake on top of it.

13. Spread the remaining icing on the top of the upper layer.

14. Garnish as desired.

15. Slice and serve.

Prep Time: 15 minutes

Cooking Time: 30 minutes

Total Time: 45 minutes

Serving: 8

Nutritional Values:

- *Calories 307*
- *Total Fat 29 g*
- *Saturated Fat 14g*
- *Cholesterol 111 mg*
- *Sodium 122 mg*
- *Total Carbs 7 g*
- *Sugar 1 g*
- *Fiber 3 g*
- *Protein 6 g*

Double layer Cream Cake

Ingredients:

First Layer

- 3 tablespoons coconut flour
- 1/4 cup erythritol, powdered
- 1 teaspoon baking powder
- 1 tablespoon gelatine
- 8 tablespoons butter
- 1/2 teaspoon vanilla essence
- 2 large eggs,

Second Layer

- 8 tablespoons butter,
- 8 oz. cream cheese,

- 1/2 teaspoon vanilla essence
- Liquid stevia, to taste
- 2 large eggs,

Method:

1. Let your oven preheat at 350 degrees F.
2. Take an 8-inch springform pan and butter it to grease well.

First layer

3. Beat vanilla and butter in all the eggs in a mixer.
4. Stir in gelatine, baking powder, flour, and gelatine.
5. Mix well until everything is well incorporated. Set this mixture aside.

Second Layer

6. Beat the butter with cream cheese separately in an electric mixer.
7. Add stevia and vanilla essence for flavor. Then whisk in eggs.
8. Beat everything until the mixture is smooth.

Assembly:

9. First spread the first layer in the greased baking pan.

10. Then top this layer with batter from the second layer evenly.

11. Bake the cake for 25 minutes in the preheated oven.

12. Once done, remove the cake from the oven and allow it to cool on wire rack,

13. Refrigerate for 2 hours in a wrapped plastic sheet.

14. Slice and serve.

Prep Time: 15 minutes

Cooking Time: 25 minutes

Total Time: 45 minutes

Serving: 8

Nutritional Values:

- *Calories 336*
- *Total Fat 34.5 g*
- *Saturated Fat 21.4 g*
- *Cholesterol 139 mg*
- *Sodium 267 mg*
- *Total Carbs 9.1 g*
- *Sugar 0.2 g*
- *Fiber 1.1 g*
- *Protein 5.1 g*

Italian Pecan Cake

Ingredients:

Cake

- 1/2 cup butter softened
- 1 cup Swerve
- 4 large eggs, separated
- 1/2 cup heavy cream
- 1 teaspoon vanilla essence
- 1 1/2 cups almond flour
- 1/2 cup coconut, shredded
- 1/2 cup pecans, chopped
- 1/4 cup coconut flour

- 2 teaspoons baking powder
- 1/2 teaspoon salt
- 1/4 teaspoon tartar cream

Frosting

- 8 ounces cream cheese softened
- 1/2 cup heavy whipping cream
- 1/2 cup butter softened
- 1 cup powdered Swerve
- 1 teaspoon vanilla essence

Garnish

- 2 tablespoons coconut, shredded lightly toasted
- 2 tablespoons pecans, chopped lightly toasted

Method:

Cake

1. Let your oven preheat at 325 degrees F.
2. Take two 8 inches baking pan and grease them with butter.
3. Beat egg yolks with cream, sweetener, butter, and vanilla in a mixed.
4. Combine all the flours, chopped pecans, salt, baking powder, and coconut shred.

5. Add this mixture to the egg yolk batter and mix well.
6. Beat egg whites separately in a mixer until foamy.
7. Fold this foamy mixture into the flour batter.
8. Now divide the batter into the baking pans.
9. Bake them for 45 minutes in the preheated oven.
10. Remove each cake from their baking pan and let them cool on the wire rack.

Frosting

11. Combine all the ingredients for frosting in a mixer until frothy.
12. Keep it aside.

To Assemble

13. First place one cake on a plate.
14. Spread a layer of half of the frosting over its top evenly.
15. Place the second cake over it and cover it with remaining frosting.
16. Garnish it with coconut shred and pecans.
17. Chill the cake in the refrigerator for 30 minutes or more to chill.
18. Slice and serve.

Prep Time: 15 minutes

Cooking Time: 45 minutes

Total Time: 60 minutes

Serving: 8

Nutritional Values:

- *Calories 267*
- *Total Fat 44.5 g*
- *Saturated Fat 17.4 g*
- *Cholesterol 153 mg*
- *Sodium 217 mg*
- *Total Carbs 8.4 g*
- *Sugar 2.3 g*
- *Fiber 1.3 g*
- *Protein 3.1 g*

Allspice Almond Cake

Ingredients:

For the cake:

- 1/2 cup erythritol
- 5 tablespoons butter softened
- 4 large eggs
- 2 tablespoons unsweetened almond milk
- 1 teaspoon vanilla
- 1 1/2 cups Almond Flour
- 2 tablespoons coconut flour
- 1 tablespoon baking powder
- 1 1/2 teaspoon cinnamon, ground

- 1/4 teaspoon ground allspice
- 1/2 cup almonds

Cream Cheese Frosting:
- 4 oz. cream cheese softened
- 2 tablespoons butter softened
- 1 teaspoon vanilla
- 1 tablespoon heavy cream
- 1/4 cup confectioners erythritol

Method:
1. Let your oven preheat at 350 degrees F.
2. Take a 9-inch pan and line it with a parchment paper.
3. Beat erythritol in butter in a suitable bowl until foamy.
4. Whisk in vanilla, eggs, and milk.
5. Beat well then stir in spices, coconut flour, almond flour, and baking powder.
6. Now add the almond to this batter and mix gently.
7. Pour the almond batter in the baking pan and spread it evenly.
8. Bake it for 25 minutes in the preheated oven.
9. Meanwhile, beat frosting ingredients in a bowl until creamy.
10. Once the cake is made, remove it from the pan and place it over a wire rack.

11. After ten minutes, spread the frosting over the cake evenly.

12. Refrigerate for 30 minutes or more.

13. Slice and serve.

Prep Time: 15 minutes

Cooking Time: 25 minutes

Total Time: 40 minutes

Serving: 8

Nutritional Values:

- *Calories 331*
- *Total Fat 38.5 g*
- *Saturated Fat 19.2 g*
- *Cholesterol 141 mg*
- *Sodium 283 mg*
- *Total Carbs 9.2 g*
- *Sugar 3 g*
- *Fiber 1 g*
- *Protein 2.1 g*

Keto bar Recipes

Crunchy Chocolate Bars

Ingredients:

- 1 1/2 cups sugar-free chocolate chips
- 1 cup almond butter
- Stevia to taste
- 1/4 cup coconut oil
- 3 cups pecans, chopped

Method:

1. Take an 8-inch baking pan and line it with parchment paper.
2. Melt chocolate chips with sweetener and coconut oil in a glass bowl.

3. Mix well then add seeds and nuts.

4. Pour this nutty batter in the baking pan.

5. Place the pan in the refrigerator for 2 hours.

6. Remove the pan and slice it into

7. Pour this batter into the baking pan and spread evenly.

8. Place it in the refrigerator for 2 hours.

9. Slice in small bars and serve.

10. Enjoy.

Prep Time: 15 minutes

Cooking Time: 0 minutes

Total Time: 15 minutes

Serving: 8

Nutritional Values:

- Calories 316
- Total Fat 30.9 g
- Saturated Fat 8.1 g
- Cholesterol 0 mg
- Sodium 8 mg
- Total Carbs 8.3 g
- Sugar 1.8 g
- Fiber 3.8 g
- Protein 6.4 g

Lemon Egg Bars

Ingredients:

- 1/2 cup butter, melted
- 1 3/4 cups almond flour
- 1 cup erythritol, powdered
- Juice from 3 medium lemons
- 3 large eggs

Method:

1. Take an 8-inch baking pan and line it with parchment paper.
2. Whisk butter with almond flour, erythritol, and salt in a suitable bowl.
3. Transfer the crumbly batter to a pan and press it firmly.
4. Bake the crust for 20 mins in the preheated oven at 350 degrees F.

5. Once the crust is done, allow it to cool for 10 minutes at room temperature.
6. Mix rest of the ingredients in a separate bowl.
7. Pour it over the baked crust and spread it evenly.
8. Again bake it for 25 minutes in the oven at the same temperature.
9. Remove the pan and slice the bars.
10. Garnish with erythritol.
11. Serve and enjoy.

Prep Time: 15 minutes
Cooking Time: 45 minutes
Total Time: 60 minutes
Serving: 8

Nutritional Values:
- *Calories 282*
- *Total Fat 25.1 g*
- *Saturated Fat 8.8 g*
- *Cholesterol 100 mg*
- *Sodium 117 mg*
- *Total Carbs 9.4 g*
- *Sugar 0.7 g*
- *Fiber 3.2 g*
- *Protein 8 g*

Caramel Bars

Ingredients:

For the Cracker Base
- 1 cup almond flour
- 1/4 teaspoon salt
- 1/4 teaspoon baking powder
- 1 egg
- 2 tablespoons grass-fed salted butter, melted

Caramel Sauce
- 1/2 cup Swerve
- 1/2 cup butter
- 1/2 cup heavy cream
- 1 teaspoon caramel extract

- 1/2 teaspoon vanilla essence
- 1/4 teaspoon salt

Toppings:
- 2 cups lily's chocolate chips
- 1 cup pecans, chopped
- 1 cup coconut, shredded

Method:

Crackers:
1. Let your oven preheat at 300 degrees F.
2. Combine baking powder, salt and almond flour in a suitable bowl.
3. Beat the butter in the egg until well combined.
4. Pour this butter mixture into the flour mixture and stir well to combine.
5. Place the dough on the working surface layered with parchment paper.
6. Cut the dough into a rectangle then cover it with a parchment paper.
7. Now spread it using a rolling pin into 1/8 inch thick dough sheet.
8. Transfer it to the baking pan and bake for 35 minutes in the preheated oven.
9. Increase the temperature of the oven to 375 degrees F.

Caramel sauce:
10. Put butter in a saucepan and melt it while mixing in swerve.

11. After boiling it for 7 minutes with stirring turn off the heat.
12. Stir in vanilla, cream and caramel extracts.
13. Once combined spread the sauce over the baked crackers base.
14. Drizzle chocolate chips, coconut, and pecans over it.
15. Bake for another 5 mins at the same temperature.
16. Remove it from the pan and allow it to cool and set.
17. Slice to serve.
18. Enjoy.

Prep Time: 15 minutes
Cooking Time: 40 minutes
Total Time: 55 minutes
Serving: 8

Nutritional Values:
- *Calories 358*
- *Total Fat 35.2 g*
- *Saturated Fat 15.2 g*
- *Cholesterol 69 mg*
- *Sodium 178 mg*
- *Total Carbs 7.4 g*
- *Sugar 1.1 g*
- *Fiber 3.5 g*
- *Protein 5.5 g*

Peanut Butter Bars

Ingredients:

Bars
- 3/4 cup almond flour
- 2 oz. butter
- 1/4 cup Swerve
- 1/2 cup peanut butter
- Vanilla 1/2 teaspoon

Topping
- 1/2 cup sugar-free chocolate chips

Method:
1. First, put all the ingredients for the bars in a suitable bowl.
2. Mix them well until properly combined.

43

3. Now spread this mixture into a 6 inch greased pan and firmly press it in.
4. Melt chocolate chips in the microwave then pour it over the bar mix.
5. Place the pan in the refrigerator for 30 mins or more until set.
6. Remove the base from pan and slice it.
7. Serve.

Prep Time: 15 minutes
Cooking Time: 0 minute
Total Time: 15 minutes
Serving: 8

Nutritional Values:
- *Calories 214*
- *Total Fat 19 g*
- *Saturated Fat 5.8 g*
- *Cholesterol 15 mg*
- *Sodium 123 mg*
- *Total Carbs 6.5 g*
- *Sugar 1.9 g*
- *Fiber 2.1 g*
- *Protein 6.5 g*

Chocolate Dipped Granola Bars

Ingredients:

- 1 egg
- 3 tablespoons coconut oil
- 1 ½ oz. almonds
- 1 oz. sesame seeds
- ¼ teaspoon flaxseed
- 1 oz. coconut, shredded, unsweetened
- 1 ½ oz. walnuts
- 1 oz. sugar-free dark chocolate
- 1 oz. pumpkin seeds
- 2 tablespoons tahini
- 1 teaspoon cinnamon, ground

- ½ pinch sea salt
- ½ teaspoon vanilla essence
- 1 ½ oz. sugar-free dark chocolate

Method:

1. Let your oven preheat at 350 degrees F.
2. Coarsely grind all the ingredients except chocolate in a food processor.
3. Spread the ground mixture in a suitable baking pan layered with wax paper.
4. Transfer the baking pan to the middle rack of the oven to bake for 20 minutes.
5. Once ready, remove the base of the bar from the pan and allow it to cool at room temperature.
6. Slice it into small squares and place them over a wire rack.
7. Melt the chocolate in a bowl in a microwave.
8. Pour this melt over the bars evenly.
9. Place the bars over a baking sheet.
10. Refrigerate them for 20 minutes until the chocolate has set.
11. Serve and enjoy.

Prep Time: 15 minutes
Cooking Time: 20 minutes

Total Time: 35 minutes

Serving: 4

Nutritional Values:

- *Calories 313*
- *Total Fat 28.4 g*
- *Saturated Fat 12.1 g*
- *Cholesterol 27 mg*
- *Sodium 39 mg*
- *Total Carbs 9.2 g*
- *Sugar 3.1 g*
- *Fiber 4.6 g*
- *Protein 8.1 g*

Lime Mixed Shortbread Bars

Ingredients:

Shortbread Crust:

- 1 1/4 cups almond flour
- 1/3 cup Swerve
- 1/4 teaspoon salt
- 1/4 cup butter melted

Key Lime Filling:

- 3 ounces cream cheese softened
- 2 teaspoons lime zest
- 4 egg yolks
- 1 cup full fat coconut milk

- 6 tablespoons key lime juice

Method:

Crust:

1. Let your oven preheat at 325 degrees F.
2. Combine sweetener with salt and almond flour in a suitable bowl.
3. Add in melted butter and then pour it in an 8inch pan.
4. Press the crust firmly and then bake it for 15 minutes in the preheated oven.
5. Once done, allow it to cool at room temperature for 15 minutes.

Lime Filling:

6. Beat the cream cheese with egg yolks and lime zest during this time.
7. Once smooth and foamy, whisk in lime juice and milk in the mixture.
8. Spread this filling in the baked crust and return the pan to the oven for 20 minutes.
9. Once done, allow it to cool for 10 minutes at room temperature.
10. Slice the base into bars then garnish as desired.
11. Enjoy.

Prep Time: 15 minutes

Cooking Time: 35 minutes

Total Time: 50 minutes

Serving: 8

Nutritional Values:

- *Calories 220*
- *Total Fat 20.1 g*
- *Saturated Fat 7.4 g*
- *Cholesterol 132 mg*
- *Sodium 157 mg*
- *Total Carbs 63 g*
- *Sugar 0.4 g*
- *Fiber 2.4 g*
- *Protein 6.1 g*

Chocolate Protein Bar

Ingredients:

- 1 cup nut butter
- 4 tablespoons coconut oil
- 2 scoops vanilla protein
- Stevia, to taste
- ½ teaspoon pink salt

Optional Ingredients:

- 4 tablespoons sugar-free chocolate chips
- 1 teaspoon cinnamon

Method:

1. Take a medium-sized dish and mix stevia, with salt, protein, butter and coconut oil.

2. Once well combined, fold in chocolate chop and cinnamon.

3. Spread this mixture into a pan and press it firmly.

4. Refrigerate it for 30 minutes to set it.

5. Slice and serve.

Prep Time: 10 minutes

Cooking Time: 0 minutes

Total Time: 10 minutes

Serving: 8

Nutritional Values:

- Calories 179
- Total Fat 15.7 g
- Saturated Fat 8 g
- Cholesterol 0 mg
- Sodium 43 mg
- Total Carbs 4.8 g
- Sugar 3.6 g
- Fiber 0.8 g
- Protein 5.6 g

Sukrin Protein Bars

Ingredients:

- 2 oz. butter
- 6 oz. Sukrin Gold Fibber Syrup
- 3 oz. thickened cream
- 3 oz. whey protein powder
- 0.4 oz. Sukrin Melis
- 1 teaspoon vanilla essence
- 1 pinch sea salt flakes

Nougat Layer

- 3 oz. Sukrin Clear Fibber Syrup
- 2 oz. whey protein isolate
- 0.4 oz. cacao powder

Method:

Caramel Layer

1. Cook all of its ingredients in a suitable glass bowl in the microwave for 2 minutes.
2. Once melted, mix well then divide the mixture into two glass bowls.
3. Heat the one half for 1 minute more in the microwave to thicken it.
4. Mix the other half with sukrin, salt, vanilla, and protein.
5. Divide it into 6 molds of a tray.
6. Top each of the molds with thickened caramel sauce.

Chocolate Layer

7. To prepare this layer, cook fiber syrup for 2 minutes in the microwave.
8. Then add protein and cacao powder to it.
9. Mix well well then pour it over the caramel layer in each mold.
10. Refrigerate it for 30 minutes or more.
11. Serve and enjoy.

Prep Time: 15 minutes
Cooking Time: 2 minutes
Total Time: 17 minutes
Serving: 8

Nutritional Values:

- *Calories 331*
- *Total Fat 32.9 g*
- *Saturated Fat 6.1 g*
- *Cholesterol 10 mg*
- *Sodium 18 mg*
- *Total Carbs 9.1 g*
- *Sugar 2.8 g*
- *Fiber 0.8 g*
- *Protein 4.4 g*

Pie and Tart Recipes

Mixed Berries Tart

Ingredients:

Tart crust:
- 2 1/4 cups almond flour
- 1/4 cup erythritol, powdered
- 5 tablespoons butter, melted
- 1/4 teaspoon sea salt

Filling
- 6 oz. mascarpone cheese
- 2 tablespoons erythritol
- 1/3 cup heavy cream

- 1 teaspoon vanilla essence
- 1/4 teaspoon lemon zest fresh

To garnish:
- 6 raspberries
- 6 blueberries
- 6 blackberries

Method:

Crust:
1. Let your oven preheat at 350 degrees F.
2. Prepare about 6 4 inch small tart pans by greasing them with butter.
3. Combine butter with almond flour, sweetener, and salt in a food processor.
4. Divide this coarse mixture into the prepared pan and press them firmly.
5. Use the fork to make a few holes in each pan.
6. Bake the tart crust for 10 minutes until golden around edges.

Filling:
7. Beat the cream with erythritol in an electric mixer for 2 minutes approximately.

8. Gradually stir in cream and continue beating until the mixture thickens.
9. Stir in lemon zest and vanilla essence.
10. Spread this filling in the baked crust of each tart pan.
11. Garnish with berries and chill for 10 minutes in the refrigerator.
12. Serve and enjoy.

Prep Time: 15 minutes
Cooking Time: 10 minutes
Total Time: 25 minutes
Serving: 8

Nutritional Values:
- *Calories 237*
- *Total Fat 22 g*
- *Saturated Fat 9 g*
- *Cholesterol 35 mg*
- *Sodium 118 mg*
- *Total Carbs 5 g*
- *Sugar 1 g*
- *Fiber 2 g*
- *Protein 5 g*

Creamy Chocolate Tart

Ingredients:

Crust

- 6 tablespoons coconut flour
- 2 tablespoons erythritol
- 4 tablespoons butter, melted
- 2 4-inch tart pans
- 1 large egg

Filling

- 2 oz. sugar-free chocolate
- 1/2 cup heavy whipping cream
- 1/4 cup erythritol, powdered
- 1 large egg

- 1 oz. cream cheese
- Liquid stevia, to taste

Method:

1. Let your oven preheat at 350 degrees F.
2. Take 2- 4 inches tart pans and grease them with butter.
3. Coarsely grind everything for the crust in a food processor.
4. Divide this mixture into each pan and press it firmly.
5. Pierce few holes in the crust using a fork.
6. Bake both the crusts for 12 minutes.
7. During this time, heat the cream in a saucepan on medium heat.
8. Fold in chocolate and cook until it melts in.
9. Use the immersion blender to puree this mixture.
10. Add egg, cream cheese, erythritol and stevia to the chocolate puree.
11. Divide this filling into each crust.
12. Return both the pans to the oven and bake at 325 degrees F for 15 minutes.
13. Place the tart pans on a wire rack to let them cool at room temperature.
14. Then transfer them to the refrigerator for 2 hours.
15. Serve and enjoy.

Prep Time: 15 minutes

Cooking Time: 27 minutes

Total Time: 42 minutes

Serving: 8

Nutritional Values:

- *Calories 190*
- *Total Fat 17.25 g*
- *Saturated Fat 7.1 g*
- *Cholesterol 20 mg*
- *Sodium 28 mg*
- *Total Carbs 5.5 g*
- *Sugar 2.8 g*
- *Fiber 3.8 g*
- *Protein 3 g*

Blackberry Lemon Tart

Ingredients:
- 1 cup lemon curd
- 1 cup blackberries
- 1 tablespoon sliced almonds
- 2 9" tart molds with loose bottoms

Almond Flour Pie Crust
- 1.5 cup blanched almond flour
- 1/2 cup coconut flour
- 4 tablespoons erythritol, powdered
- 2 eggs
- 4 tablespoons cold butter, unsalted

Method:
1. Let your oven preheat at 350 degrees F.

2. Prepare the dough by mixing everything for pie crust.
3. Divide the dough into two equal sized balls.
4. Take two tart molds and layer it with foil and parchment paper.
5. Spread one dough ball into each pan and press it evenly.
6. Make a few holes into each dough layer using a fork.
7. Bake the tart crusts for 15 mins in the preheated oven.
8. Place the tart pans on a wire pan to cool the crust at room temperature.
9. Fill both the crusts with lemon curd equally.
10. Top it with berries, erythritol and almond slices.
11. Serve and enjoy.

Prep Time: 15 minutes
Cooking Time: 15 minutes
Total Time: 30 minutes
Serving: 8

Nutritional Values:
- *Calories 321*
- *Total Fat 12.9 g*
- *Saturated Fat 5.1 g*
- *Cholesterol 17 mg*
- *Sodium 28 mg*
- *Total Carbs 8.1 g*
- *Sugar 1.8 g*
- *Fiber 0.4 g*
- *Protein 5.4 g*

Strawberry Vanilla Tart

Ingredients:

Coconut crust:
- 1/2 cup coconut oil
- 3/4 cup 2 tablespoons coconut flour
- 2 eggs
- 1 teaspoon vanilla essence
- 1 teaspoon powdered sweetener

Cream Filling:
- 1 cup mascarpone
- 2 eggs separated

- 1 teaspoon vanilla essence
- 1-2 tablespoons powdered sweetener
- 1 cup strawberries

Method:

Crust:

1. Let your oven preheat at 350 degrees F.
2. Beat eggs in a suitable bowl then add rest of the ingredients.
3. Spread this dough in between two sheets of parchment paper.
4. Place this dough sheet in a greased pan and pierce holes in it using a fork.
5. Bake this crust for 10 minutes in the preheated oven.

Cream Filling:

6. Beat the egg whites in an electric mixer until frothy.
7. Stir in mascarpone cream, egg yolks, sweetener, and vanilla and beat for 2 minutes.
8. Spread this filling in the baked crust evenly.
9. Top the filling with the sweetener and strawberries.
10. Place the pie in the refrigerator for 30 minutes.
11. Slice and serve.

Prep Time: 15 minutes
Cooking Time: 10 minutes

Total Time: 25 minutes

Serving: 8

Nutritional Values:

- *Calories 236*
- *Total Fat 21.5 g*
- *Saturated Fat 15.2 g*
- *Cholesterol 54 mg*
- *Sodium 21 mg*
- *Total Carbs 7.6 g*
- *Sugar 1.4 g*
- *Fiber 3.8 g*
- Protein 4.3 g

Blueberry Lemon Filling Tart

Ingredients:

Crust:

- 1 cup superfine almond flour
- 2 tablespoons swerve
- 3/4 teaspoon baking powder
- 1 pinch sea salt
- 1 teaspoon vanilla essence
- 4 tablespoons extra cold butter

Filling:

- 8-ounce cream cheese
- 3 tablespoons erythritol

- 1 large egg
- 1/2 teaspoon lemon essence
- 1 teaspoon lemon zest fresh

Topping:

- 1 cup blueberries fresh or frozen

Method:

1. Blend butter with salt, almond flour, and erythritol in a suitable bowl.
2. Spread this mixture in an 8inch pan layered with wax paper.
3. Bake the tart crust for 20 minutes in a preheated oven at 350 degrees.
4. Place the crust pan on wire rack for 10 minutes to cool at room temperature.
5. Whisk lemon juice, lemon zest, ¾ cup almond flour, salt, and ¾ cup erythritol.
6. Once combined, pour this mixture into the baked crust and spread it evenly.
7. Return the pan to the oven again for 25 minutes at the same temperature.
8. Garnish with blueberries.
9. Serve and enjoy.

Prep Time: 15 minutes

Cooking Time: 25 minutes

Total Time: 40 minutes

Serving: 8

Nutritional Values:

- *Calories 367*
- *Total Fat 35.1 g*
- *Saturated Fat 10.1 g*
- *Cholesterol 12 mg*
- *Sodium 48 mg*
- *Total Carbs 8.9 g*
- *Sugar 3.8 g*
- *Fiber 2.1 g*
- *Protein 6.3 g*

Cheesecake Jam Tarts

Ingredients:

Crust

- 3 tablespoons butter, melted
- ¾ cup almond flour

Filling

- 12 oz. cream cheese,
- 1 egg
- ¼ cup erythritol
- 1 teaspoon vanilla essence
- 1 tablespoon fresh lemon juice
- ¼ teaspoon salt

Toppings

- ¼ cup sugar-free strawberry jam
- ¼ cup blueberries

Method:

1. Let your oven preheat at
2. Preheat your oven to 350 degrees F.
3. Mix almond flour with butter in a bowl.
4. Divide this mixture into the muffin tin and press it firmly.
5. Bake for 8 minutes until golden brown.
6. Meanwhile, beat cream cheese in an electric mixture along with 1 egg.
7. Beat in erythritol, vanilla essence, salt, and lemon juice and mix well.
8. Divide this filling into the muffin crust.
9. Bake the mini tarts for 20 minutes, then allow it to cool
10. Top with jam and blueberries.
11. Refrigerate overnight then Serve.

Prep Time: 15 minutes
Cooking Time: 28 minutes
Total Time: 43 minutes
Serving: 8

Nutritional Values:

- *Calories 175*
- *Total Fat 16 g*
- *Saturated Fat 2.1 g*
- *Cholesterol 0 mg*
- *Sodium 8 mg*
- *Total Carbs 2.8 g*
- *Sugar 1.8 g*
- *Fiber 0.4 g*
- *Protein 9 g*

Pumpkin Almond Pie

Ingredients:

Almond Flour Pie Crust

- 2 cups almond flour
- 4 tablespoons butter, melted
- 1 teaspoon vanilla
- 1 egg yolk
- ½ teaspoon cinnamon

Pumpkin Spice Filling

- 8 ounces cream cheese
- 1 cup heavy cream
- 4 eggs
- 1 teaspoon vanilla

- 2 teaspoons pumpkin pie spice
- ¼ teaspoon salt
- ⅔ cups Swerve (Confectioners)

Method:

1. Put everything for the crust in a suitable bowl.
2. Spread and press this mixture into a pie pan.
3. Bake this crust for 12 minutes in a preheated oven at 400 degrees F.

Filling

4. Beat eggs in the cream cheese until it turns frothy.
5. Add rest of the ingredients to the cream cheese and stir well to combine.
6. Spread this filling into the baked crust evenly.
7. Return the stuffed pie to the oven and bake for another 45 minutes at the same temperature.
8. Place the hot pie on a wire rack to cool for 10 minutes.
9. Garnish with almond or as desired.
10. Slice and enjoy.

Prep Time: 15 minutes
Cooking Time: 57 minutes
Total Time: 72 minutes
Serving: 8

Nutritional Values:

- *Calories 285*
- *Total Fat 27.3 g*
- *Saturated Fat 14.5 g*
- *Cholesterol 175 mg*
- *Sodium 165 mg*
- *Total Carbs 3.5 g*
- *Sugar 0.4 g*
- *Fiber 0.9 g*
- *Protein 7.2 g*

Almond Meal Vanilla Tart

Ingredients:

Crust

- 1 tablespoon swerve
- 6 teaspoons flaxseed meal
- 1/4 teaspoon nutmeg
- 1/2 oz. butter, unsalted, melted
- 6 tablespoons almond meal
- 1/2 egg

Filling

- 1/2 vanilla bean
- 1 egg

- 1 egg yolk
- 1 1/4 tablespoon erythritol
- 3/4 cup whipping cream

Method:
1. Let the oven preheat at 350 degrees F.
2. Mix everything or the crust in a suitable bowl.
3. Spread and press this mixture in a greased pie pan.
4. Bake this crust for 12 minutes in the preheated oven at 350 degrees F.
5. Once done, keep the crust at room temperature to cool.

Filling
6. Decrease the temperature of the oven to 320 degrees F.
7. Beat the vanilla seeds, swerve and egg yolks in eggs using a mixer.
8. Whisk in cream and stir well until smooth.
9. Pour this filling through a sieve and discard the vanilla seeds.
10. Spread this filling into the baked crust and return the pan to the oven.
11. Bake it again for 25 minutes approximately.
12. Allow the baked pie to cool at room temperature for 10 minutes.

13. Drizzle nutmeg on top then refrigerate for 30 minutes to chill.
14. Slice and enjoy.

Prep Time: 15 minutes
Cooking Time: 25 minutes
Total Time: 40 minutes
Serving: 4

Nutritional Values:

- *Calories 215*
- *Total Fat 20 g*
- *Saturated Fat 7 g*
- *Cholesterol 38 mg*
- *Sodium 12 mg*
- *Total Carbs 8 g*
- *Sugar 1 g*
- *Fiber 6 g*
- *Protein 5 g*

Cookie Recipes

Chocolate Chip Butter Cookies

Ingredients:
- ¼ cup coconut flour
- ⅓ cup butter, unsalted
- 3 tablespoons Swerve
- 2 eggs, large
- 3 tablespoons sugar-free chocolate chips
- ¼ teaspoon vanilla essence
- ⅛ teaspoon salt

Method:
1. Mix salt, swerve and coconut flour in a suitable bowl.
2. Beat the vanilla essence and butter in egg in a mixer.

3. Stir in the sweetened flour mixture and mix well to combine.
4. Fold in chocolate chips then drop this batter spoon by spoon on a cookie sheet.
5. Make as many cookies to use the complete batter.
6. Bake the set cookies in the preheated oven for 15 mins at 350 degrees F.
7. Let them cool first then serve.

Prep Time: 10 minutes
Cooking Time: 15 minutes
Total Time: 25 minutes
Serving: 8

Nutritional Values:
- *Calories 198*
- *Total Fat 19.2 g*
- *Saturated Fat 11.5 g*
- *Cholesterol 123 mg*
- *Sodium 142 mg*
- *Total Carbs 4.5 g*
- *Sugar 3.3 g*
- *Fiber 0.3 g*
- *Protein 3.4 g*

Vanilla Shortbread Cookies

Ingredients:

- 2 1/2 cups almond flour
- 6 tablespoons butter
- 1/2 cup erythritol
- 1 teaspoon vanilla essence

Method:

1. Let your oven preheat at 350 degrees F.
2. Spread a parchment paper in a cookie sheet.
3. Beat erythritol in the butter until it turns frothy.
4. Add in flour and vanilla essence while beating the mixture.

5. Divide this batter on a cookie sheet in small cookies.
6. Bake those cookies for 15 mins in the preheated oven at 350 degrees F.
7. Serve and enjoy.

Prep Time: 10 minutes
Cooking Time: 15 minutes
Total Time: 25 minutes
Serving: 6

Nutritional Values:
- *Calories 288*
- *Total Fat 25.3 g*
- *Saturated Fat 6.7 g*
- *Cholesterol 23 mg*
- *Sodium 74 mg*
- *Total Carbs 9.6 g*
- *Sugar 0.1 g*
- *Fiber 3.8 g*
- *Protein 7.6 g*

Cream Dipped Cookies

Ingredients:
- 1 cup almond flour
- ½ cup cacao nibs
- ½ cup coconut flakes, unsweetened
- 1/3 cup erythritol
- ½ cup almond butter
- ¼ cup butter, melted
- 2 large eggs
- Stevia, to taste
- ¼ teaspoon salt

Glaze:
- ¼ cup heavy whipping cream
- 1/8 teaspoon xanthan gum

- Stevia, to taste
- Optional: ½ teaspoon vanilla essence

Method:

1. Let your oven preheat at 350 degrees F.
2. Combine all the dry ingredients in a suitably sized bowl.
3. Beat stevia, almond butter, butter, and vanilla essence in the eggs.
4. Stir in the almond flour mixture and whisk well.
5. Make 16 cookies on a cookie sheet by dropping the batter spoon by spoon.
6. Press each cookie to flatten it.
7. Bake them for 25 mins in the preheated oven.
8. During this time, combine the glaze ingredients in a saucepan.
9. Let them cook until the sauce thickens.
10. Once the cookies are done, place them over the wire rack.
11. Pour this cooked glaze over the cookies equally.
12. Allow this glaze to set in 15 minutes.
13. Enjoy.

Prep Time: 15 minutes
Cooking Time: 25 minutes
Total Time: 40 minutes
Serving: 8

Nutritional Values:

- *Calories 192*
- *Total Fat 17.44 g*
- *Saturated Fat 11.5 g*
- *Cholesterol 125 mg*
- *Sodium 135 mg*
- *Total Carbs 2.2 g*
- *Sugar 1.4 g*
- *Fiber 2.1 g*
- *Protein 4.7 g*

Nutmeg Gingersnap Cookies

Ingredients:

- 2 cups almond flour
- ¼ cup butter, unsalted
- 1 cup erythritol
- 1 large egg
- 1 teaspoon vanilla essence
- ¼ teaspoon salt
- 2 teaspoons ground ginger
- ¼ teaspoon ground nutmeg
- ¼ teaspoon ground cloves
- ½ teaspoon cinnamon, ground

Method:

1. Let the oven preheat at 350 degrees F.
2. Spread the parchment paper on a cookie sheet
3. First, beat the wet ingredients in an electric mixer.
4. Then stir in everything else and mix until smooth.
5. Divide the dough into small cookies on the cookie sheet spoon by spoon.
6. Bake them for 12 mins in the preheated oven.
7. Enjoy.

Prep Time: 10 minutes
Cooking Time: 12 minutes
Total Time: 22 minutes
Serving: 8

Nutritional Values:

*   Calories 77.88
*   Total Fat 7.13 g
*   Saturated Fat 4.5 g
*   Cholesterol 15 mg
*   Sodium 15 mg
*   Total Carbs 0.8 g
*   Sugar 0.2 g
*   Fiber 0.3 g
*   Protein 2.3 g

Buttery Energy Bites

Ingredients:

- 1 cup almond flour
- 3 tablespoons butter
- 2 tablespoons erythritol
- 1 teaspoon vanilla essence
- pinch of salt

Method:

1. Put all the ingredients in a suitable bowl.
2. Whisk this mixture until well combined.
3. Divide the cookie dough into small cookies on a baking sheet.

4. Place the cookie/baking sheet in the refrigerator to chill for 1 hour.

5. Enjoy after bringing it to room temperature.

Prep Time: 15 minutes
Cooking Time: 0 minutes
Total Time: 15 minutes
Serving: 8

Nutritional Values:

- Calories 114
- Total Fat 9.6 g
- Saturated Fat 4.5 g
- Cholesterol 10 mg
- Sodium 155 mg
- Total Carbs 3.1 g
- Sugar 1.4 g
- Fiber 1.5 g
- Protein 3.5 g

Cinnamon Snickerdoodle Balls

Ingredients:

Cookies:

- 2 eggs
- 2 teaspoons vanilla essence
- 1 cup almond butter
- 1/2 cup almond milk
- 1/4 cup coconut oil, solid, at
- 1 1/2 cup monk fruit sweetener
- 1 3/4 cup almond flour
- 1 cup coconut flour
- 1 teaspoon baking soda

- 2 teaspoons tartar cream
- 1/8 teaspoon pink Himalayan salt
- 1 teaspoon cinnamon

Topping:

- 3 tablespoons monk fruit sweetener
- 1 tablespoon cinnamon

Method:

1. Let your oven preheat at 350 degrees F.
2. Line a cookie sheet with wax paper.
3. Add the wet ingredients of the cookies to a blender and beat well.
4. Stir in dry mixture and combine them well.
5. Place this batter in the refrigerator for 15 minutes to set.
6. Make small balls out of this mixture.
7. Mix cinnamon and monk fruit in a shallow plate.
8. Roll these balls into this mixture to coat well.
9. Bake these balls in a baking sheet for 12 minutes.
10. Serve once cooled.

Prep Time: 10 minutes
Cooking Time: 12 minutes
Total Time: 22 minutes
Serving: 8

Nutritional Values:

- Calories 252
- Total Fat 17.3 g
- Saturated Fat 11.5 g
- Cholesterol 141 mg
- Sodium 153 mg
- Total Carbs 7.2 g
- Sugar 0.3 g
- Fiber 1.4 g
- Protein 5.2 g

Vanilla Cream Cheese Cookies

Ingredients:

- 1/4 cup butter
- 2 oz. plain cream cheese
- 1/2 cup erythritol
- 1 large egg white
- 2 teaspoons vanilla essence
- 3 cup almond flour
- 1/4 teaspoon sea salt

Method:

1. Let your oven preheat at 350 degrees F.
2. Line a cookie sheet with wax paper.

3. Blend butter, cream cheese, egg white and vanilla essence in a blender.
4. Add flour, erythritol, and salt, and mix well until smooth.
5. Divide the dough into small cookies on the cookie sheet.
6. Bake for 15 mins in the preheated oven.
7. Allow the cookies to cool in 15 minutes.
8. Serve.

Prep Time: 15 minutes
Cooking Time: 15 minutes
Total Time: 30 minutes
Serving: 8

Nutritional Values:

- Calories 195
- Total Fat 14.3 g
- Saturated Fat 10.5 g
- Cholesterol 175 mg
- Sodium 125 mg
- Total Carbs 4.5 g
- Sugar 0.5 g
- Fiber 0.3 g
- Protein 3.2 g

Coconut Vanilla Cookies

Ingredients:

- 6 tablespoons coconut flour
- ¾ teaspoon baking powder
- 1/8 teaspoon salt
- 3 tablespoons butter
- 1/6 cup coconut oil
- 6 tablespoons swerve
- 2 large eggs
- 1/2 tablespoon coconut milk
- 1/2 teaspoon vanilla essence

Method:

1. Let your oven preheat at 375 degrees F.
2. Line a baking sheet with wax paper.

3. Beat all the wet ingredients in a food processor.
4. Stir in rest of the ingredients and mix well.
5. Divide the dough into small cookies on the cookie sheet.
6. Bake for 10 mins in the preheated oven.
7. Allow the cookies to cool in 15 minutes.
8. Serve.

Prep Time: 10 minutes
Cooking Time: 10 minutes
Total Time: 20 minutes
Serving: 4

Nutritional Values:

- *Calories 151*
- *Total Fat 14.7 g*
- *Saturated Fat 1.5 g*
- *Cholesterol 13 mg*
- *Sodium 53 mg*
- *Total Carbs 1.5 g*
- *Sugar 0.3 g*
- *Fiber 0.1 g*
- *Protein 0.8 g*

Candy and Confections

Raspberry Fat Bombs

Ingredients:

- 1 cup coconut butter
- 1 cup of coconut milk
- ½ cup of coconut oil
- ¼ cup cacao butter
- 1 teaspoon vanilla essence
- ¼ cup freeze-dried raspberries
- Stevia to taste

Method:
1. Place the paper liners in the muffin cups of a tray.

2. Cook everything in a saucepan for 2 minutes on medium heat.
3. Mix well then allow it to cool for 5 minutes.
4. Divide the mixture into the muffin cups.
5. Place one raspberry on top of each muffin.
6. Then keep the muffin tray in the refrigerator for 3 hours.
7. Remove the fat bombs from the muffin cups.
8. Serve.

Prep Time: 15 minutes
Cooking Time: 0 minutes
Total Time: 15 minutes
Serving: 12

Nutritional Values:

- *Calories 261*
- *Total Fat 27.1 g*
- *Saturated Fat 23.4 g*
- *Cholesterol 0 mg*
- *Sodium 10 mg*
- *Total Carbs 6.1 g*
- *Sugar 2.1 g*
- *Fiber 3.9 g*
- *Protein 1.8 g*

Peppermint Candies

Ingredients:

- 1/2 cup coconut butter
- 1/4 cup unsweetened coconut, shredded
- 2 tablespoons coconut oil
- 1 teaspoon peppermint extract
- Erythritol to taste
- 4 oz. sugar-free dark chocolate
- 4 tablespoons coconut oil

Method:

1. First, melt the coconut butter in a saucepan.
2. Add 2 tbsp coconut oil, peppermint, stevia and coconut shreds.

3. Cook this mixture until well heated and mixed.
4. Let it cool for 5 mins then divide it into small muffin cups.
5. Place the muffin cups in the refrigerator for 1 hour.
6. Meanwhile, melt the dark chocolate and 4 tbsp coconut oil in a microwave.
7. Pour this mixture into the muffin cups.
8. Let them again cool in the refrigerator for 1 hour.
9. Remove the candies from the cups and enjoy.

Prep Time: 15 minutes

Cooking Time: 3 minutes

Total Time: 18 minutes

Serving: 12

Nutritional Values:

- *Calories 139*
- *Total Fat 4.6 g*
- *Saturated Fat 0.5 g*
- *Cholesterol 1.2 mg*
- *Sodium 83 mg*
- *Total Carbs 7.5 g*
- *Sugar 6.3 g*
- *Fiber 0.6 g*
- *Protein 3.8 g*

Cocoa Peppermint Fat Bombs

Ingredients:

- 2 tablespoons coconut oil melted
- 1 tablespoon swerve
- 1/4 teaspoon peppermint essence
- 2 tablespoons cocoa unsweetened

Method:

1. Mix swerve with peppermint and coconut oil in a suitable bowl.
2. Divide half of this mixture in an ice cube tray.
3. Place the tray in the refrigerator for 1 hour.
4. Add cocoa powder to the reserved mixture and mix well.
5. Pour it over the refrigerated candies.

6. Return the tray to the refrigerator again for 30 minutes.
7. Remove the candies from the tray.
8. Serve.

Prep Time: 15 minutes
Cooking Time: 2 minutes
Total Time: 17 minutes
Serving: 8

Nutritional Values:

- *Calories 200*
- *Total Fat 21.1 g*
- *Saturated Fat 19.5 g*
- *Cholesterol 14.2 mg*
- *Sodium 46 mg*
- *Total Carbs 1.1 g*
- *Sugar 1.3 g*
- *Fiber 0.4 g*
- *Protein 0.4 g*

Coconut Tea Candy

Ingredients:

- 2 cups black tea
- 3 tablespoons coconut milk
- Stevia, to taste
- 5 tablespoons gelatine powder

Method:

1. Take a saucepan and mix the stevia, coconut milk and black tea in it.
2. Cook this mixture to a mixture then add gelatin.
3. After mixing it well enough, pass it through a sieve.
4. Divide the candy mixture into silicone candy molds.

5. Place the candy tray in the refrigerator for 2 hours.

6. Once set, remove the candies from the molds.

7. Serve and enjoy.

Prep Time: 15 minutes

Cooking Time: 5 minutes

Total Time: 20 minutes

Serving: 8

Nutritional Values:

- *Calories 136*
- *Total Fat 10.7 g*
- *Saturated Fat 0.5 g*
- *Cholesterol 4 mg*
- *Sodium 45 mg*
- *Total Carbs 1.2 g*
- *Sugar 1.4 g*
- *Fiber 0 g*
- *Protein 0. g*

Cucumber and Lime Sweets

Ingredients:

- 1 cucumber, peeled
- 15-20 fresh mint leaves
- 1/2 lime juice
- 1.5 tablespoons gelatine powder
- stevia, to taste

Method:

1. Add stevia, cucumber, mint and lime juices in a blender.
2. Blend these ingredients for a minute.
3. Strain this puree over a saucepan to get its liquid.
4. Cook this liquid to a simmer, then stir in gelatine powder.
5. Once well combined, turn off the heat.

6. Pour this mixture into a silicon candy tray.

7. Place this tray in the refrigerator for 2 hours.

8. Remove the candies from their molds and serve.

Prep Time: 15 minutes

Cooking Time: 5 minutes

Total Time: 20 minutes

Serving: 4

Nutritional Values:

- *Calories 91*
- *Total Fat 4.7 g*
- *Saturated Fat 0.8 g*
- *Cholesterol 11 mg*
- *Sodium 43 mg*
- *Total Carbs 0 g*
- *Sugar 0.2 g*
- *Fiber 0.5 g*
- *Protein 2 g*

Hibiscus Gelatin Gummies

Ingredients:

- 1 3/4 cup hot water
- 3 passion tea bags
- 6 tablespoons grass fed gelatine

Method:

1. Pour water in a saucepan and cook it to boil then turn off the heat.

2. Place the tea bags in hot water and steep them for 10 minutes.

3. Remove the tea bags from the water.

4. Mix gelatine powder in ½ cup of tea water.

5. Return the remaining tea water to the heat.

6. Let this water heat then stir in gelatine mixture.

7. Stir cook for 1 minute then divides the mixture into a candy mold tray.

8. Place this tray in the refrigerator for 1 hour.

9. Remove the candies from the molds.

10. Enjoy.

Prep Time: 15 minutes

Cooking Time: 5 minutes

Total Time: 20 minutes

Serving: 4

Nutritional Values:

- *Calories 38*
- *Total Fat 0.6 g*
- *Saturated Fat 0 g*
- *Cholesterol 0 mg*
- *Sodium 33 mg*
- *Total Carbs 0 g*
- *Sugar 0 g*
- *Fiber 0 g*
- *Protein 9 g*

Turmeric Milk Gummies

Ingredients:

- ¼ cup of water
- 3 tablespoons gelatine
- 1 cup of coconut milk
- 1 teaspoon turmeric
- ½ teaspoon ginger
- Pinch of freshly ground black pepper
- Pinch of cardamom powder
- Liquid stevia, to taste

Method:

1. Combine gelatine with water in a saucepan by stirring it well.

2. Heat milk in another saucepan and stir in all the spices on medium heat.
3. After cooking the spiced milk for 5 mins turn off the heat.
4. Add stevia to the milk then pour this mixture into the gelatine mixture.
5. Mix it all well, then pour it into candy molds.
6. Place the molds in the refrigerator for 3 hours.
7. Remove the candies from the molds.
8. Serve and enjoy.

Prep Time: 15 minutes
Cooking Time: 5 minutes
Total Time: 20 minutes
Serving: 8

Nutritional Values:

- *Calories 76*
- *Total Fat 7.2 g*
- *Saturated Fat 6.4 g*
- *Cholesterol 0 mg*
- *Sodium 8 mg*
- *Total Carbs 2g*
- *Sugar 1 g*
- *Fiber 0.7 g*
- *Protein 2.2 g*

Cinnamon Pecans Candies

Ingredients:

- 1 cup erythritol
- 1 lb. pecan halves
- 1 egg white
- 1 tablespoon water
- 2 teaspoons cinnamon, ground
- 2 teaspoons ground nutmeg
- 1 teaspoon salt
- Baking spray or butter

Optional

- 1 teaspoon pumpkin pie spice
- Erythritol, to taste

Method:

1. Let the oven preheat at 250 degrees F.
2. Combine the dry ingredients in a suitable bowl.
3. Beat egg white with a tablespoon of water until frothy using a mixer.
4. Stir in the dry mixture along with pecans.
5. Mix well to coat all the pecans well.
6. Spread the pecans on a baking sheet.
7. Place this sheet in the preheated oven for 15 minutes.
8. Allow them to cool for a few minutes.
9. Serve.

Prep Time: 10 minutes

Cooking Time: 15 minutes

Total Time: 25 minutes

Serving: 8

Nutritional Values:

- *Calories 193*
- *Total Fat 20 g*
- *Saturated Fat 13.2 g*
- *Cholesterol 10 mg*
- *Sodium 8 mg*
- *Total Carbs 2.5 g*
- *Sugar 1 g*
- *Fiber 0.7 g*
- *Protein 2.2 g*

Frozen Desserts

Vanilla Yogurt

Ingredients:
- 1 vanilla pod (seeds)
- 1 teaspoon vanilla essence
- 1 13.5-ounce can full-fat coconut milk
- Erythritol, to taste
- 1/4 teaspoon salt
- 1/4 teaspoon xanthan gum
- 1 cup of coconut yogurt
- 2 teaspoons vanilla essence
- 1 tablespoon vodka

Method:
1. Combine salt, coconut milk, erythritol and vanilla seeds in a saucepan.

2. Cook this milk mixture for 15 minutes on medium heat.
3. Stir in xanthan gum and whisk this mixture until frothy.
4. Strain it through a sieve in a to bowl then cover the mixture with a plastic wrap.
5. Place the bowl for 30 minutes in the refrigerator.
6. Add yogurt to a suitable bowl then add the refrigerator vanilla mixture and vanilla essence.
7. Mix well and churn it in an ice cream maker for 20 minutes.
8. Freeze it for 2 hours in the freezer then transfer it to a covered container.
9. Place it back in the refrigerator for 6 hours.
10. Serve and enjoy.

Prep Time: 15 minutes
Cooking Time: 15 minutes
Total Time: 30 minutes
Serving: 4

Nutritional Values:
- *Calories 173*
- *Total Fat 13 g*
- *Saturated Fat 10.1 g*
- *Cholesterol 12 mg*
- *Sodium 67 mg*
- *Total Carbs 7.5 g*
- *Sugar 1.2 g*
- *Fiber 0.6 g*
- *Protein 3.2 g*

Mango yogurt popsicles

Ingredients:

- 8 oz. frozen mango, diced
- 8 oz. frozen strawberries
- 1 cup Greek yogurt
- 2.5 teaspoons heavy whipping cream
- 1 teaspoon vanilla essence

Method

1. Beat everything in a food processor until it forms a smooth batter.
2. Divide this mixture into the popsicle molds.

3. Cover the molds and stick the popsicle sticks into the molds.
4. Place the popsicle in the freezer for 4 hours.
5. Remove the popsicle from the molds.
6. Serve and enjoy.

Prep Time: 15 minutes
Cooking Time: 0 minutes
Total Time: 15 minutes
Serving: 4

Nutritional Values:
- *Calories 197*
- *Total Fat 19.2 g*
- *Saturated Fat 10.1 g*
- *Cholesterol 11 mg*
- *Sodium 78 mg*
- *Total Carbs 7.3 g*
- *Sugar 1.2 g*
- *Fiber 0.8 g*
- *Protein 4.2 g*

Protein yogurt

Ingredients:

- 1 cup Greek yogurt full-fat
- 1 cup raspberries frozen
- 1 tablespoon coconut oil
- 1 tablespoon vanilla whey powder
- Stevia extract to taste
- 1 dash salt
- 1 tablespoon vodka optional - to taste

Method

1. Beat everything in a food processor until smooth.
2. Transfer the yogurt mixture to a sealable bowl.

3. Place it in the freezer for about 4 hours.
4. Serve and enjoy.

Prep Time: 15 minutes

Cooking Time: 0 minutes

Total Time: 15 minutes

Serving: 4

Nutritional Values:

- *Calories 213*
- *Total Fat 19 g*
- *Saturated Fat 15.2 g*
- *Cholesterol 13 mg*
- *Sodium 52 mg*
- *Total Carbs 5.5 g*
- *Sugar 1.3 g*
- *Fiber 0.5 g*
- *Protein 6.1 g*

Cocoa Yogurt Ice Cream

Ingredients:

- 2½ oz. fat-free Greek yogurt
- ½ oz. vanilla protein powder
- 1 teaspoon unsweetened cocoa powder
- ½ cup unsweetened almond milk
- 1 teaspoon vanilla essence
- Stevia to taste
- Almonds & berries (optional)

Method

1. Beat everything in a food processor until smooth.
2. Transfer the yogurt mixture to a sealable bowl.
3. Place the mixture in the freezer for about 4 hours.

4. During this time, churn this ice cream in an ice cream maker after every 30 minutes.
5. Garnish with berries and almonds.
6. Serve.

Prep Time: 15 minutes
Cooking Time: 0 minutes
Total Time: 15 minutes
Serving: 4

Nutritional Values:
- *Calories 117*
- *Total Fat 21.2 g*
- *Saturated Fat 10.4 g*
- *Cholesterol 19.7 mg*
- *Sodium 104 mg*
- *Total Carbs 7.3 g*
- *Sugar 3.4 g*
- *Fiber 2 g*
- *Protein 8.1 g*

Frozen yogurt with Berries

Ingredients:

- 4 cups frozen blackberries
- 1 cup full-fat Greek yogurt
- 1 tablespoon lemon juice
- 1 teaspoon vanilla essence

Method

1. Beat everything in a food processor until smooth.
2. Transfer the yogurt mixture to a sealable bowl.
3. Place it in the freezer overnight.
4. Serve and enjoy.

Prep Time: 15 minutes

Cooking Time: 0 minutes

Total Time: 15 minutes

Serving: 4

Nutritional Values:

- *Calories 113*
- *Total Fat 9 g*
- *Saturated Fat 0.2 g*
- *Cholesterol 1.7 mg*
- *Sodium 134 mg*
- *Total Carbs 6.5 g*
- *Sugar 1.8 g*
- *Fiber 0.7 g*
- *Protein 7.5 g*

Raspberry Ice cream

Ingredients:

- 2 cups frozen raspberries unsweetened
- 1 cup full-fat Greek yogurt
- Powdered Swerve, to taste

Method:

1. Beat everything in a food processor until smooth.
2. Transfer the yogurt mixture to a sealable bowl.
3. Place the mixture in the freezer for about 4 hours.
4. During this time, churn this ice cream in an ice cream maker after every 30 minutes.
5. Serve.

Prep Time: 15 minutes

Cooking Time: 0 minutes

Total Time: 15 minutes

Serving: 3

Nutritional Values:

- *Calories 101*
- *Total Fat 15.5 g*
- *Saturated Fat 4.5 g*
- *Cholesterol 12 mg*
- *Sodium 18 mg*
- *Total Carbs 4.4 g*
- *Sugar 1.2 g*
- *Fiber 0.3 g*
- *Protein 4.8 g*

Creamy Avocado Dessert

Ingredients:

- 1 avocado, peeled, pitted, and diced
- 1/4 cup heavy whipping cream
- Liquid stevia, to taste
- 1/4 teaspoon vanilla essence
- 1/4 teaspoon cinnamon, ground

Method:

1. Beat everything in a food processor until smooth.
2. Transfer the yogurt mixture to a sealable bowl.

3. Place the mixture in the freezer for about 1 hour.

4. Serve and enjoy.

Prep Time: 15 minutes

Cooking Time: 0 minutes

Total Time: 15 minutes

Serving: 4

Nutritional Values:

- *Calories 266*
- *Total Fat 25.7 g*
- *Saturated Fat 1.2 g*
- *Cholesterol 41 mg*
- *Sodium 18 mg*
- *Total Carbs 9.7 g*
- *Sugar 1.2 g*
- *Fiber 0.5 g*
- *Protein 2.6 g*

Cheesecake Vanilla Bites

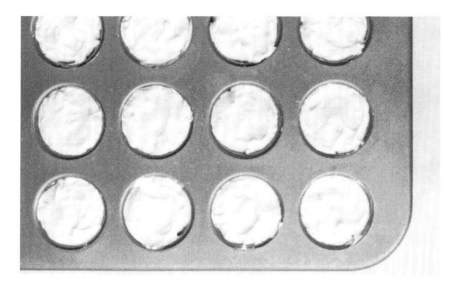

Ingredients:

- 8 oz. cream cheese softened
- 1/2 cup butter softened
- 1/2 cup erythritol or sugar substitute
- 1/2 teaspoon vanilla essence

Method

1. Beat everything in a food processor until smooth.
2. Line a baking sheet with parchment paper.
3. Divide the mixture into a muffin tray.
4. Place the tray in the freezer for 1 hour.
5. Serve and enjoy.

Prep Time: 15 minutes

Cooking Time: 0 minutes

Total Time: 15 minutes

Serving: 4

Nutritional Values:

- *Calories 147*
- *Total Fat 11 g*
- *Saturated Fat 10.1 g*
- *Cholesterol 10 mg*
- *Sodium 91 mg*
- *Total Carbs 4.2 g*
- *Sugar 2 g*
- *Fiber 0.4 g*
- *Protein 3.2 g*

Custard or Mousse Recipes

Vanilla custard with Pecan

Ingredients:

- 6 egg yolks
- ½ cup unsweetened almond milk
- 1 teaspoon vanilla essence
- 1 teaspoon erythritol
- ¼ cup melted coconut oil or butter, unsalted
- 2 tablespoons pecans, chopped

Method:

1. Beat vanilla, sweetener, egg yolks in almond milk in a suitable bowl.

2. Add in the fat and whisk well to combine.

3. Meanwhile, cook the water to a boil in a large pot.

4. Place the egg bowl over the boiling water carefully.

5. Let it stir cook for 5 minutes.

6. Remove the bowl from the pot and fold in pecans.

7. Transfer it to the serving dish.

8. Place the dish in the refrigerate for 2 hours.

9. Serve.

Prep Time: 15 minutes

Cooking Time: 10 minutes

Total Time: 25 minutes

Serving: 4

Nutritional Values:

- *Calories 243*
- *Total Fat 21 g*
- *Saturated Fat 18.2 g*
- *Cholesterol 121 mg*
- *Sodium 34 mg*
- *Total Carbs 7.3 g*
- *Sugar 0.9 g*
- *Fiber 0.1 g*
- *Protein 4.3 g*

Lemon Cream Custard

Ingredients:

- 1/2 cup almond milk
- 1 cup thickened cream
- 2 teaspoons lemon essence
- 4 egg yolks
- 1 teaspoon xanthan gum
- 1/3 cup erythritol

Method:

1. Whisk cream with milk in a saucepan over medium heat.
2. Stir in lemon essence and cook the mixture to a boil.
3. Then let it simmer for 5 minutes.

4. Beat erythritol, xanthan gum in egg yolks over in a suitable bowl.
5. Pour in the cream mixture with constant stirring.
6. Again cook this mixture for 20 minutes in the same saucepan.
7. Allow it to cool at room temperature than in the refrigerator.
8. Serve.

Prep Time: 15 minutes
Cooking Time: 40 minutes
Total Time: 55 minutes
Serving: 4

Nutritional Values:
- *Calories 183*
- *Total Fat 15 g*
- *Saturated Fat 12.1 g*
- *Cholesterol 11 mg*
- *Sodium 31 mg*
- *Total Carbs 6.2 g*
- *Sugar 1.6 g*
- *Fiber 0.8 g*
- *Protein 4.5 g*

Vanilla Bean Custard

Ingredients:

- 2 cups pure cream
- 6 egg yolks, large
- 2 tablespoons sweetener
- 1 vanilla bean
- 1 pinch salt

Method:

1. Whisk the cream with seeds, salt, and vanilla beans in a saucepan.
2. First, cook this mixture to a boil.
3. Meanwhile, beat the sweetener in the egg yolks in a suitable bowl.

4. Gradually stir in the boiled cream mixture while mixing well.

5. Pour the custard back to the same saucepan and cook until it thickens.

6. Strain it to remove the vanilla pod.

7. Refrigerate it to chill.

8. Enjoy.

Prep Time: 15 minutes

Cooking Time: 15 minutes

Total Time: 30 minutes

Serving: 5

Nutritional Values:

- *Calories 388*
- *Total Fat 31 g*
- *Saturated Fat 12.2 g*
- *Cholesterol 101 mg*
- *Sodium 54 mg*
- *Total Carbs 3 g*
- *Sugar 1.3 g*
- *Fiber 0.6 g*
- *Protein 5 g*

Vanilla Crème Brûlée

Ingredients:
- 2 cups heavy cream
- 5 egg yolks
- 6 tablespoons erythritol
- 1 pinch salt
- 1 vanilla bean

Topping
- 3 tablespoons erythritol

Method:
1. Let your oven preheat at 360 degrees F.
2. Start by boiling the cream in a saucepan then add vanilla bean.

3. After cooking for 3 minutes then add whisked egg yolks, salt, and erythritol.
4. Strain this mixture in a baking dish to remove the vanilla.
5. Bake this Brulee for 15 minutes in the preheated oven.
6. Let it cool first at room temperature then place in the refrigerate to chill.
7. Dig in!

Prep Time: 15 minutes
Cooking Time: 15 minutes
Total Time: 30 minutes
Serving: 4

Nutritional Values:
- Calories 153
- Total Fat 13 g
- Saturated Fat 9.2 g
- Cholesterol 6.5 mg
- Sodium 81 mg
- Total Carbs 4.5 g
- Sugar 1.4 g
- Fiber 0.4 g
- Protein 5.8 g

Coconut Chocolate Mousse

Ingredients:

- 1 cup heavy whipping cream
- 3 tablespoons raw cacao powder
- 1/2 teaspoon cinnamon
- Stevia extract, to taste
- Toasted flaked coconut or almonds for garnish

Method:

1. Beat cream with cacao powder in a suitable bowl until fluffy.
2. Stir in cinnamon and stevia.

3. Combine well then garnish with coconut.
4. Enjoy.

Prep Time: 5 minutes
Cooking Time: 0 minutes
Total Time: 5 minutes
Serving: 4

Nutritional Values:

- *Calories 254*
- *Total Fat 09 g*
- *Saturated Fat 10.1 g*
- *Cholesterol 13 mg*
- *Sodium 179 mg*
- *Total Carbs 7.5 g*
- *Sugar 1.2 g*
- *Fiber 0.8 g*
- *Protein 7.5 g*

Raspberry Pecan Mousse

Ingredients

- 1 teaspoon lemon zest

- 3 oz. raspberries or blueberries

- 2 oz. pecans, chopped

- ¼ teaspoon vanilla essence

- 2 cups whipping cream

Method

1. Beat the cream in a mixer until it is fluffy.

2. Add lemon zest and vanilla, stir well to combine.

3. Fold in berries and chopped pecans.

4. Cover the mousse bowl with plastic wrap.

5. Place the bowl in the refrigerator for 3 hours.

6. Garnish with raspberries or as desired.

7. Serve.

Prep Time: 15 minutes

Cooking Time: 0 minutes

Total Time: 15 minutes

Serving: 4

Nutritional Values:

- *Calories 265*
- *Total Fat 13 g*
- *Saturated Fat 10.2 g*
- *Cholesterol 09 mg*
- *Sodium 7.1 mg*
- *Total Carbs 7.5 g*
- *Sugar 1.1 g*
- *Fiber 0.5 g*
- *Protein 5.2 g*

Cocoa Mocha Mousse

Ingredients:

Cream cheese mixture:

- 8 ounces cream cheese, softened
- 3 tablespoons sour cream
- 2 tablespoons butter, softened
- 1 ½ teaspoons vanilla essence
- 1/3 cup erythritol
- ¼ cup unsweetened cocoa powder
- 3 teaspoons instant coffee powder

Whipped cream mixture:

- 2/3 cup heavy whipping cream
- 1 ½ teaspoons erythritol

- ½ teaspoon vanilla essence

Method:
1. Whisk cream cheese with sour cream and butter in a mixer.
2. Add coffee powder, vanilla, sweetener, and cocoa powder.
3. Mell well and set this mixture aside.
4. Beat the rest of the ingredients then add that mixture to the whisked cream cheese.
5. Cover the bowl and place it in the refrigerator for 2 hours.
6. Serve and enjoy.

Prep Time: 15 minutes
Cooking Time: 0 minutes
Total Time: 15 minutes
Serving: 4

Nutritional Values:
- Calories 290
- Total Fat 21.5 g
- Saturated Fat 15.2 g
- Cholesterol 12.1 mg
- Sodium 9 mg
- Total Carbs 6.5 g
- Sugar 1.2 g
- Fiber 0.4 g
- Protein 6.2 g

Conclusion

Perhaps it is now safe to say that we can enjoy some amazingly sweet recipe on a complete ketogenic diet without actually having any carbohydrates. With all these recipes, of various variety, your keto dessert menu will become full of colors and flavors. With a good understanding of the low carb sweetener and keto substitutes, anyone can enjoy these delectable delights right at home. Just be more vigil while using certain ingredients like the chocolates, flours, and sweeteners, always read their labels to counter check the carb content, since not all companies ensure the standard carb quantity for low carb diet.

32487140R00080

Made in the USA
San Bernardino, CA
15 April 2019